What Do You See?

Jan Swartz

Illustrated by Randol Eagles

Dominie Press, Inc.

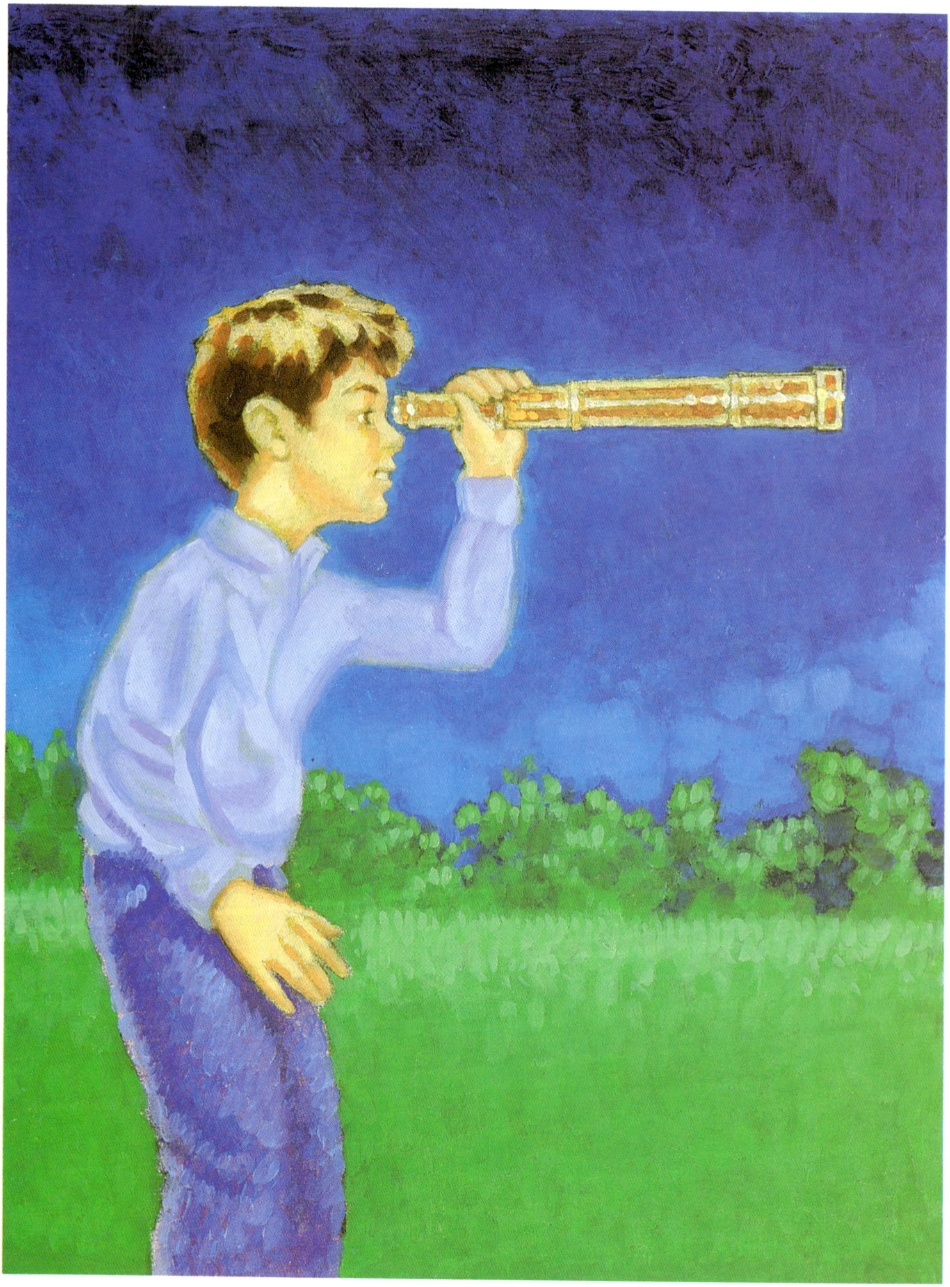

What do you see?

4

I see the stars.

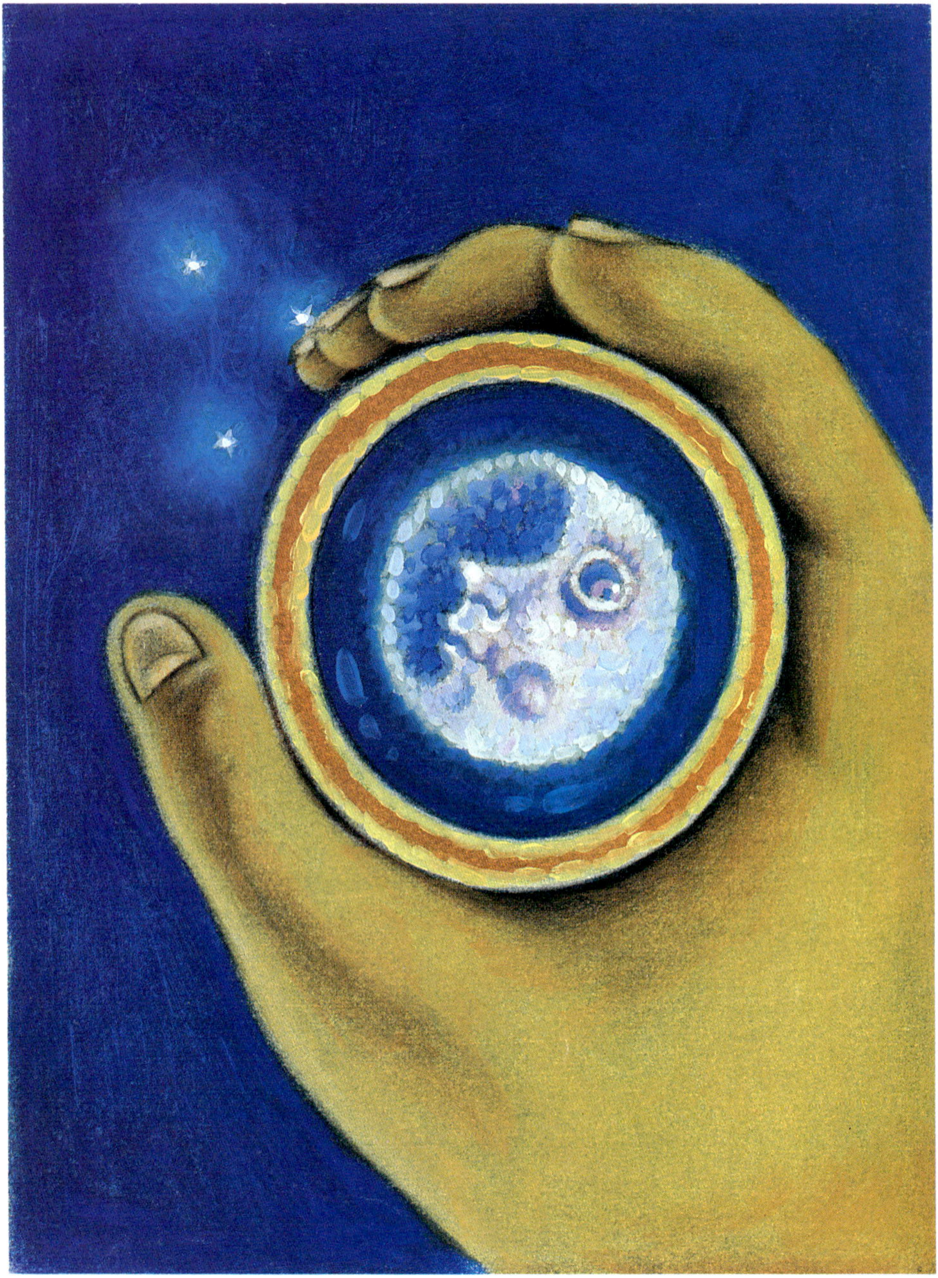

I see the moon.

8

I see a planet.

I see the sky.

The development of the *Carousel Readers* was supported by the Reading Recovery project at California State University, San Bernardino. All authors' royalties from the sale of the *Carousel Readers* will be used to support various Reading Recovery projects.

Publisher: Raymond Yuen
Illustrator: Randol Eagles
Cover Designer: Pamela Pettigrew-Norquist

Copyright © 1994 Dominie Press, Inc.

All rights reserved. No part of this publication may be reproduced or transmitted in any form or by any means without permission in writing from the publisher. Reproduction of any part of this book, through photocopy, recording, or any electronic or mechanical retrieval system, without the written permission of the publisher is an infringement of the copyright law.

Published by

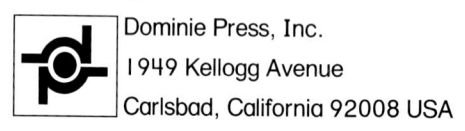

Dominie Press, Inc.
1949 Kellogg Avenue
Carlsbad, California 92008 USA

ISBN 1-56270-206-8
Printed in Singapore by PH Productions Pte Ltd.

7 IP 99